Nicholas Alexander Hayes

Amorphous Organics

SurVision Books

First published in 2020 by
SurVision Books
Dublin, Ireland
Reggio di Calabria, Italy
www.survisionmagazine.com

Copyright © Nicholas Alexander Hayes, 2020

Cover images: photos of La casa orgánica, Mexico;
                architect Javier Senosiain

Design © SurVision Books, 2020

ISBN: 978-1-912963-10-2

This book is in copyright. No part of this publication may be reproduced, stored in a retrieval system, or transmitted in any form or by any means without the prior permission in writing from the publisher.

Acknowledgments

Grateful acknowledgment is made to the editors of the following, in which some of these poems, or versions of them, originally appeared, or are about to appear:

Former Cactus: "The Divorce" (as "A Body Rebels")

Peculiar Mormyrid: "Homunculi", "Worms", and "A Pleasant, Sunny Day"

Sein und Werden: "Under Snow"

SurVision: [East decides...], [Tongues roll...], "A Minor Procedure", "An Exam", and "If It Quivers"

Contents

Talk West	5
Purifying Unas in the Jackal Lake	6
[East decides...]	7
Panspermia	8
Common Ancestor	9
The Divorce	10
[Tongues roll...]	11
A Minor Procedure	12
An Exam	13
[Intestines decide...]	14
[The toenail...]	15
A Happiness You Can Find	16
Returning to the Black Spot	17
[A man feels...]	18
[A man cups...]	19
Homunculi	20
[Horses gallop...]	21
The Wheel	22
Worms	23
Fieldnotes on Turdus Migratorius	24
A Pleasant, Sunny Day	26
Carnicería Los Monarcas	28
Under Snow	30
If It Quivers	31

Talk West

Typos are the lexicographical equivalent of hobos. Willfully free from the square lives of bourgeois words that insist on living in sentences gently divorced from their neighbors by fences of white paper and sternly posted punctuation. Typos wander through this landscape loving each other in the shadows of the jungle fire. Letting their musky, potbellied love rub out all manner of pleasures and meanings against each other. The salty gestures done, they rinse their mouths with some MD 20/20 or Everclear. Perhaps they will travel with their companions for a spell down the track, but they must always know they are alone. It is the only way to evade the bulls who are ready to tussle and bludgeon them with Wite-Out.

Purifying Unas in the Jackal Lake

Sitting on the bathtub's edge, frail tenuous psyche puts its head in its hands and massages its silvery translucent temples in an effort to waylay the imminent migraine.

As the ba waits for release, it leaps from the bathtub to the back of the toilet where it nibbles on the corners of glossy magazines.

The body hangs on towel hooks behind the door. Slack it waits to dry from the delicate wash it has been put through. It resists itself, falling forward and setting into folds and pained recesses.

The ba brushes against the body making a purring sound that rolls off its parasite tongue.

[East decides...]

East decides to become north. He sidles over, nudging his brother out of bed. But north clinging to the comforter drags east to the floor. Sobbing and slapping each other, their tumult leads them to drift away from Earth. South and west nestled at the foot of the bed do not notice their siblings' absence but feel a chill.

Panspermia

Strike your cane against
the void to see
manna
flow

sweet like
divinity cooling on the
breezeway on a
clear winter day

in yellow fields
encroached by locust thickets.

Cup your hand below
my beard to
see if you can
hold a swarm,

a pestilence
of unspoken words

of lost affectations.

Common Ancestor

the common ancestor of the mollusk —
an unspeaking tongue —
lolling out from deep time.

a peristaltic vein
connecting us as it
drives us forward
embedding us in history's soft walls.

facing erosion
some may be jealous
of the nacre encrusted
few who dislodge themselves

and pass on
through venal chambers,
waiting to be harvested

and dropped into a lonely
champagne flute under
iron stars.

The Divorce

A body has become an ocean floor not by choice, but its components have rebelled, wanting to return to their primordial state before they had been duped into symbiotic coexistence. Ribs split from each other and bloom as branches of coral. The heart becomes a red puffer fish skimming and playing between polyps. Lungs loving their union spread like a ray and bide their time on the floor with the vertebrae who now use nerve tissue as tube worms to be a part of the world but removed from it not being able to bear disunion. Most of the other organs will find themselves shells, so they can exist as bivalves ready to be shucked and slurped down with some cold mignonette. Flesh surrenders itself to being a sea of carnal sea grass. Feeling defeated, other bones render themselves sand. All regress but the skull and brain which feel betrayed. They dive deep to take solace with the coelacanth.

[Tongues roll...]

Tongues roll off the pier. They are rushing for the ship that has already departed. The cool breeze and bright sun make the autumn day seem kind, but they obscure the monolingual famine. Tongues roll off the pier splashing in the murky water of the bay. They writhe through rainbow oil spots trying to make it to the ship where their brethren urge them on from the deck with promises of more substantial fare of dental fricatives and lingual ingresses.

A Minor Procedure

The appendix indexes itself. Solemnly placing itself in the file between appendage and apprentice, it knows it will be missed. It leaks through the cardboard sleeve. Pus and gore drop to the bottom of the cabinet. The lack of pain will make the body long for it. It is certain; it is certain. It wraps some fragments of appendicular artery around itself like a scarf before crying itself to sleep.

An Exam

Gossamer clogs the arteries of a middle-aged man. Cardiologists use machetes to clear a path through the aorta. They proceed with trepidation feeling the perilous weakness in the ground thanks to an aneurysm. One missteps, and his boot breaks through, dangling in space. But he is pulled through safely. They continue cutting their way to the heart. An irregular murmur makes them feel uncomfortable. They are relieved by a sudden chill. They are only hearing ghosts and not defect.

[Intestines decide...]

Intestines decide it's their turn to shine. The brain and heart have had their time to be the headline organ. The stomach always a solid best friend to the lead. They call their agent and demand a better role. They call the press to let them know they will be publicly running away. Perhaps some play by the tabloids will let them launch a solo career. They slop their way from the teenager's anus and grab the keys to his parent's Land Rover. They squirm their way outside and slide toward the vehicle to the rhythmic crackle of flash bulbs.

[The toenail...]

The toenail bides its times. Gnawed on by a frat boy, flexible and drunk. No dignity in the presence of the muscled and flatulent host. Its body torn off and spit into the puke stained carpet, it waits. Later when the world is still, ice trolls will creep from the internet and deliver it to the underworld. The unheroic dead will shape and place each fragment in the dragon boat Naglfar. One day the world will end, and it will sail to Valhalla so the meek and cowardly might burn the great hall down.

A Happiness You Can Find

He cut the fingers from his rings and let them dangle free in the air. Gold circles chased his hands as he conducted the baroque record that welled in the background of his dark apartment. He began to sing for finer things but nothing was quite as glorious as the table turning. Fingers flailed on the floor before regaining their composure and dragging themselves toward a small hole in the baseboard of an internal wall. They left trails of blood on the low pile camel-colored carpet.

Returning to the Black Spot

Buccaneers bury a cache of emeralds and rubies in a man's tight anus. They trust the hemorrhoids to keep the treasure safe although they leak precious fluids. The seadogs don't worry about the humming birds and butterflies that swarm them as they hazard the treacherous moss-tufted defile that leads back to their ship. These creatures are here to sip a man's sweet nectar. Some insects exhausted from fluttering hook their feet on a dingleberry until they can return to the air. The birds in constant motion flash green and red in waning daylight.

[A man feels...]

A man feels an ache in his molars before all of his teeth tumble out. They tinkle on marble tile. He hasn't seen a dentist since high school and that was twenty years ago. He won't go now because teeth are a silly atavistic vanity. He drives to the county in the middle of the night to sneak into a stable. It is quick work with a razor to trim off a horse's fore hooves. He crams these into his mouth and secures them with nails. He never liked to run his mouth before, but now it will only gallop.

[A man cups...]

A man cups a knot of butter between his palms. He licks his teeth frantically trying to see if they are loose. His body heat starts to soften the butter, and he feels the world start to slip. Crouching on the stoop, he becomes a gargoyle only to become stone. How else does one become permanent? The butter continues to melt.

Homunculi

(I)

A man cuts his finger on his tooth as he brushes his teeth. From the jagged laceration, microscopic men fall. They punch each other, knocking off their tiny fedoras. As they plummet into the sink, some are killed on impact. Others drown in frothy, minty spittle. And still others sulk around the drain despondent because Jessica has put them in the friend-zone. A speck of toothpaste makes the dolorous wound sing.

(II)

In the candle licked dusk, naked Colin Farrell calls for his cat. "Good kitty, good puss, puss, puss." He feels his fullness coursing through his body with a pronounced lilt. It oozes out of his pores, each drop of sweat containing a homunculus. Each falls to the tile floor and gains its feet. Tiny hands wipe amniotic fluid from muscular assess. Their tiny voices join Colin's. "Good kitty, good, puss, puss, puss." They feel their fullness coursing through their bodies with a pronounced lilt. It oozes out of their pores, each drop of sweat containing a smaller homunculus. Each falls to the floor and joins the search until desire is spent and the cat is abandoned.

[Horses gallop...]

Horses gallop down a woman's throat. The dust they kick up and the loose stool they drop as they race toward the stomach make her sneeze. The riders struggle to make sure that glottal trepidation doesn't force their mounts to tumble and break legs.

As they approach the esophageal sphincter, some of the more impetuous begin to fire shots into the tissue until their mounts finally leap and splash down into an acid filled bag. They race around a blockage where the US has set up a forward base. The horsemen become more strategic in their shooting. The Unitedstatesian troops stage a strategic retreat through the pyloric sphincter.

The woman feels queasy, but accepts her fate – the inevitable consequence of calling in the cavalry.

The Wheel

Carousel horses revolt. They spit out their plastic bits that have been molded to their fiberglass teeth. They tear themselves from the poles that go right through their rib cages. Gashed and rent, they stumble toward the edge of the rotating platform letting their bodies crash into the cement below. The spinning increases as a recorded pipe organ is turned up so that their whinging and plaintive neighing is drowned out. Hopes twitch, and painted eyes dart around the cage looking at the children standing in line. The rabbit, seahorse and dragon remain in place. Celestially ordained, they figure their motions are the embodiment of order. The carousel slows. Passengers are forced to leave so new riders can enter. The orbit begins again. The horses continue to twitch. The tiger looks down at the carnage hungering but unwilling to leave the wheel of life.

Worms

(I)

Gut worms build a cottage on the banks of a stream of partially digested matter. It is not always easy to live off blood and bile, so they dredge night earth and fertilize a small plot of land. They grow cabbage and Swedish turnips, healthy durable crops. After a hard day of tilling and sowing, they slither back to their round daub house to rest. But before they can sleep, they hear a knock on the door. The duke has come to demand his right of primae noctis.

(II)

Worms hold a congress in the gut. They call for independence from their host. They are tired of being lured out the anus with a bowl of milk. "Barricade the bowels and burrow into the bloodstream," cry the younger. The older are smug knowing if their bodies are ravaged and rent they will grow two from one.

Fieldnotes on Turdus Migratorius

(I)
Robins believe themselves incarnations of the Emperor's celestial guards. They line the shady neighborhood sidewalk. Near motionless, they reminisce about rivers of mercury across which the imperial family lounges in a pleasure palace until the guards can restore order to heaven and earth. One of them kills a snail—is this a barbarian invader? A cardinal—her plumage burning like a nearly extinguished ember walks between their columns—has the empress returned to earth?

(II)
A robin stands in the underbrush, flicking the tip of its switch blade then folding it back with his wing. The back of the blade bends against a deck of cards he carries with him. He hopes to menace. He wants you to think that he has a hog idling nearby. But he is only threatening worms with a game of 52 pickup.

(III)
The robin feels like it has been online for too long. It sees the world as flat planes on which illuminated objects trace themselves offering subjects that are always out of reach. The robin looks down at its chubby feathered stomach and cranes its slate colored head around the room. It opens the yellow beak to call out but no sound comes. It has been on the recliner for who knows how long binge-watching program after program until it has lost track of action and character. It has moved nothing but its eyes. Shitting unconsciously, the mess falling through legs of the recliner and slowly building up until the chair has become entombed in a guano stalagmite. It tries to call. It tries to reach for the remote to tell the TV that it is still watching.

(IV)
The early bird catches some shrapnel, and strategically retreats to rebuild itself with rubbish. Early in spring, resources are scarce. The robin crouches in its nest, affixing cardboard pieces to its wings to stabilize its flight and wraps copper wiring around its feet creating spurs to shiv other singing folk. Lastly in its mouth it grafts a half-living worm to the root of its beak. Having lost a tongue, the bird will need something to speak. Deliciousness makes it salivate. The yellow beak foams with desires never completely fulfilled.

A Pleasant, Sunny Day

The farmer has an abscessed tooth and leans against a desiccated bull, slaughtered by a man of faith for not drawing a black upright piano from the earth. Blue smoke emerges from the piano. Tongues of flame snap the strings.

Glorious and frazzled, hair cascades over his forehead in long tendrils like oozing entities that striate the ground with black and blue vascular lines. Crusty rheum collects in his crows' feet like salted soil. Varicose veins marble the industrious clay of flesh, forced to be fallow, deprived of the long and slow edge of a plow.

In the field, black berry briars and intestines creep through the branches to form a pergola. The descendant colons are an extension of the solar anus waiting to be coaxed open by the gentle pulsations of lay lines that crisscross the surface of the earth.

Furless mice with sharp wings like those of kestrels emerge from the piano smoke. Their ears have devolved into their skulls. They ride the warm current up towards the solar abyss, the solar anus. They soar between the salted earth and sour green satellite.

Under the pergola, boys and girls in bonnets sit in their bare undifferentiated bodies, covered in filth and black berry juice, having tea parties with rabid hares that hold dime store china cups in their forepaws and knock the rims of the cups with their teeth. The fertility of the earth is all that anyone worries about.

Mice circle above them in the celestial skull, the brain pain and chamber pot of the infinite. The farmer knows that the universe is excreta and the flora that grows on it is just a cycle. He can stand under the distended rectum and bowel waiting for the universe to give birth to itself, marking time by the ache of his tooth.

Carnicería Los Monarcas

Casting calm shadows in the brilliant day, a glider over traffic came.

This graceful beast sailing on stiff wings—orange fires sealed in black piping—sought to pass lean men who lurked outside a dusty deli, huddled, trading snaps, trading beats. Above the young men, the papery creature's flight arched toward an alley, overflowing with trash glistening in oily ooze. But one punk bent his powerful legs, tensed his thighs, prepared to pounce—thirst and sobriety worming from the bottom of his belly.

Neither before nor after did the flier find a faster force against it. Deprived of calm momentum, the creature crashed into the cruel boy's curved chest. Its dark wings were seized, black edges gripped by red gold hands. Shear black and shimmering orange scales stained his white Sean Jean shirt. Driven by gentle wind, the wings beat, bending around his broad shoulders. Blunt claws on spindly legs stressed soft fabric, getting caught in sagging sweat-sodden denim.

The youth forced his prey toward the storefront—fat mauve sausages were painted on the filthy glass. He pulled the hefty bug inside the gloomy store; he slipped on worn linoleum. He struggled with the light, flapping bulk.

At the display case—empty of all cuts—the clerk, in a jacket with black stains, leaned.

His hand darted toward the depressed ring between the beast's body and head. A quick fist cracked the exoskeleton, causing oil to ooze. The clerk gently laid the limp beast on the long counter. He pulled a bottle from beneath the counter. The thirsty boy took the Key Lime MD 20/20. Cracking the seal, he guzzled the green, leaving enough to share.

Under Snow

Mrs. Clusius in a dusty housecoat and a thin gold chain, that desiccated visitor with sparse white hair tucked under a canary turban emblazoned with a rhinestone broach, that anemic blossom whose waxy stalk thrusts through cedar mulch, through manured soil loosely packed around her mass of bulbs and glands wrapped in papery husk, seizes her husband's discolored hand, bidding him farewell, urging him to hobble over the path, into the warmth of the kitchen.

Mr. Clusius on the path in scuffed and holey penny loafers, polished as well as arthritis permitted—his graying socks moist from the large feathering snowflakes melting on the cobblestones—steadies his gaze on his perennial wife, watching the snow building in the folds of her turban, the fiery streaks that spread up her chest and lick her soft chin—a fungal infection that lent value to her ancestors before the development of durable cultivars.

If It Quivers

If it quivers on the desk in the studio in the morning light, filtered through gray film on the window,

If it quivers in the gray amniotic sack laced with red veins and blue arteries,

If it quivers when your hand draws near to pick up the coffee mug you sat beside it,

If it quivers as it starts to leak ichor that soddens your paper causing the ink to run,

If it quivers, anticipating your touch, you know it was never truly yours.

More poetry published by SurVision Books

Noelle Kocot. *Humanity*
(New Poetics: USA)
ISBN 978-1-9995903-0-7

Ciaran O'Driscoll. *The Speaking Trees*
(New Poetics: Ireland)
ISBN 978-1-9995903-1-4

Helen Ivory. *Maps of the Abandoned City*
(New Poetics: England)
ISBN 978-1-912963-04-1

Elin O'Hara Slavick. *Cameramouth*
(New Poetics: USA)
ISBN 978-1-9995903-4-5

John W. Sexton. *Inverted Night*
(New Poetics: Ireland)
ISBN 978-1-912963-05-8

Afric McGlinchey. *Invisible Insane*
(New Poetics: Ireland)
ISBN 978-1-9995903-3-8

Anatoly Kudryavitsky. *Stowaway*
(New Poetics: Ireland)
ISBN 978-1-9995903-2-1

Tim Murphy. *The Cacti Do Not Move*
(New Poetics: Ireland)
ISBN 978-1-912963-07-2

Tony Kitt. *The Magic Phlute*
(New Poetics: Ireland)
ISBN 978-1-912963-08-9

Clayre Benzadón. *Liminal Zenith*
(New Poetics: USA)
ISBN 978-1-912963-11-9

George Kalamaras. *That Moment of Wept*
ISBN 978-1-9995903-7-6

Anton Yakovlev. *Chronos Dines Alone*
(Winner of James Tate Poetry Prize 2018)
ISBN 978-1-912963-01-0

Bob Lucky. *Conversation Starters in a Language No One Speaks*
(Winner of James Tate Poetry Prize 2018)
ISBN 978-1-912963-00-3

Christopher Prewitt. *Paradise Hammer*
(Winner of James Tate Poetry Prize 2018)
ISBN 978-1-9995903-9-0

Mikko Harvey & Jake Bauer. *Idaho Falls*
(Winner of James Tate Poetry Prize 2018)
ISBN 978-1-912963-02-7

Tony Bailie. *Mountain Under Heaven*
(Winner of James Tate Poetry Prize 2019)
ISBN 978-1-912963-09-6

Maria Grazia Calandrone. *Fossils*
Translated from Italian
(New Poetics: Italy)
ISBN 978-1-9995903-6-9

Sergey Biryukov. *Transformations*
Translated from Russian
(New Poetics: Russia)
ISBN 978-1-9995903-5-2

Alexander Korotko. *Irrazionalismo*
Translated from Russian
(New Poetics: Ukraine)
ISBN 978-1-912963-06-5

Anton G. Leitner. *Selected Poems 1981–2015*
Translated from German
ISBN 978-1-9995903-8-3

All our books are available to order via
http://survisionmagazine.com/books.htm

www.ingramcontent.com/pod-product-compliance
Lightning Source LLC
Chambersburg PA
CBHW061314040426
42444CB00010B/2632